MY BOOK OF Grammar

GREG BLACKMAN
Dip. Teach., BEd., M.A. (Ed.), MACE.

P
· PARRAGON ·

OTHER TITLES IN THIS SERIES:

My Book of Spelling
My Book of Tables
My Book of Simple Maths
My Book of Interesting Facts

Published 1997 by Parragon,
Units 13-17, Avonbridge Trading Estate,
Atlantic Road, Avonmouth, Bristol BS11 9QD.

Copyright © 1996 The Book Company International.

ISBN 0-75252-361-9

Design by Robyn Latimer.
Printed in Italy.
All rights reserved.

P
PARRAGON

Contents

Introduction

Grammar and punctuation are the key elements to writing. Without a good understanding of them our writing would be difficult to read and understand. This book gives a sound background in the important aspects of grammar and punctuation with activities for practice.

Parts of Speech

Understanding the different parts of speech makes our writing easier and more interesting to read.
Example:
  The car left the building.
  The vivid red, sports car sped rapidly out of the building, screeching his tyres at every corner.

  The second sentence is much more interesting to read and provides a clearer picture. This is the way we should be trying to write all the time.

Nouns

Nouns are words that name a person, place or thing. There are four types; common, proper, collective, and abstract.

Common Nouns

Common nouns are words that name ordinary items that can be touched or seen.

Example:
The **desk** is in the **study.**
The **boy** climbed the **hill.**
It was a bright blue **car.**
Is that a portable **computer**?
The **sky** clouded over very quickly.

Activity
Underline the common nouns in these sentences.
1. We went to the beach and played with the ball.
2. The boy climbed over the gate and was chased by a bull.
3. The girls had a party to celebrate leaving school.
4. Each chair had to have a matching cushion.

Proper Nouns

Proper nouns are special nouns that name a particular person, place or thing. Proper nouns always start with a capital letter.

Example:

Sarah went to **Sydney** to shop.

We spent **Christmas Day** at **Darling Harbour.**

Captain Cook explored the east coast of **New Zealand.**

Mr Simpson is the coach of the **Australian Cricket Team.**

Max walked all the way back to camp and told **Mr Smith** that the group was lost.

Activity

Underline the Proper nouns in these sentences.

1. Jenny and David took their younger brother to Taronga Zoo.
2. Captain Cook explored much of the South Pacific Ocean and discovered the east coast of Australia.
3. The fire surrounded the tiny township of Louth.
4. Elton John will be performing at the Sydney Entertainment Centre tonight.

Collective Nouns

Collective nouns are names of groups of people or things.

Example:
   The **flock** of birds flew over the lake.
   The **class** enjoyed the excursion to the snow.
   The **convoy** of trucks caused a traffic jam.
   I ate the whole **bunch** of bananas in a week.
   The **band** played all night while the **audience** danced all night.

Activity
Underline the collective nouns in these sentences.
1. The swarm of bees buzzed around my head.
2. The school of fish were all caught in the net.
3. The battalion charged the enemy and suffered many casualties.
4. The pride of lions looked harmless but the crowd knew they would attack if they disturbed them.

Abstract Nouns

Abstract nouns are feelings and emotions; i.e. most things that can be felt.

Example:

The boy fell in **love** at first sight.

I value our **friendship.**

The boy's **childhood** was full of happiness.

His **greed** was disappointing.

Her natural **beauty** made her a very successful model.

Activity

Underline the abstract nouns in these sentences.

1. The boys had a lot of fun at Luna Park on Saturday.
2. We had no idea who committed the murder in the video until right at the end.
3. It is a pity we had to leave early.
4. The exhilaration we felt as we plummeted down the roller coaster was indescribable.

Noun Revision Activity

(A) Underline and then name the nouns by writing a small C (common nouns), P (proper nouns), Col (collective nouns) and an A (abstract nouns) for the following sentences.

1. The young boy sent his friend a new comic for his birthday.

2. The Headmaster gave a talk to the class about honesty.

3. Mr Jones was a butcher and bought a chain of stores called "Pete's Meat".

(B) Match the correct noun with the space.

> litter, boat, squadron, freedom, Indonesia, September, tents, annoyance.

Soldiers fight to ensure we have _____ .
A neighbour of Australia is _____ .
We camp in _____ .
A _____ of aeroplanes.

9

Adjectives

Adjectives are words that describe nouns and pronouns. They describe how many, how much, what colour, what kind, what position.

Adjectives help to provide a better picture of the nouns and pronouns they describe.

Example:
  We need **four** children to play this game.
  It was **very** late when we returned.
  The water was a brilliant **blue.**
  The house was very **spacious.**
  Michelle came **first.**

Activity:
(A) Underline the adjectives in the following sentences.

1. The seven girls went out for dinner and came home very late.
2. The shiny red convertible sped along the new highway.
3. The third boy was totally exhausted, but he ignored the extreme pain and finished the race.
4. The young boy wanted a new mountain bike for his tenth birthday.

Verbs

Verbs are action words. They tell us what the nouns or pronouns are doing. Verbs can be simple or compound.

Simple Verbs

A simple verb is a one word verb.
Example:
  Don't **play** on the steps.
  I **drew** this picture.
  I **was** there.

Compound Verbs

A compound verb is a verb that has more than one word.
Example:
  I **am going** home.
  He **has been lying** to you.
  She **will be performing** soon.

Activity
Underline the verb in these sentences and write an **S** (Simple verb) or a **C** (Compound verb) above the verb.

1. The train chugged along the tracks as the thieves rode their horses alongside.

2. He will be allowed to go out tonight.

3. Dad has made me a new cubby house.

4. Both our school teams were beaten in the first
round of the knock-out competition.

Finite Verbs

Finite verbs are verbs that have a subject. A sentence
is not a proper sentence unless it has a finite verb in
it. To find out if a verb is finite ask the question, Who
or What (verb).If you get an answer that is the
subject and the verb is finite.

Example:
The boy crashed his bike.
The verb is crashed. Ask, who or what crashed?
The answer is the boy. Therefore the verb crashed is
finite as it has a subject, the boy.

Activity
Underline the verb and then write an **s** above the
subject in the following sentences. Remember to ask
who or what about the verb.

1. The boy rode his bike down the hill.

2. The boat sank very quickly.

3. Katherine came to the library with me.

4. We smashed through the barrier.

Tense

When we talk about verbs we often talk about the tense of the verb. Tense indicates when the action occurred. It could have happened in the <u>past</u>; it could be happening now, in the <u>present</u>; or it could be going to happen in the <u>future</u>.

Past Tense

Example:
  She **swam** yesterday.
  We **danced** all night.
  I **walked** to school today.

Present Tense

Example:
  John **is riding** his bike.
  I **am leaving** now.
  The boys **are eating** lunch.

Future Tense

Example:
  I will be leaving tomorrow.
  She **will be training** all day.
  They **may win** the raffle.

Your tense in a piece of writing should remain the same. This means if you start writing in the past tense, then the whole piece of writing should be in the past tense.

Activity
(A) Underline the verbs and write the tense at the end of the sentence for the following:
1. The boy sang beautifully.
2. The girls are playing water polo.
3. The excavators discovered a fossil of a dinosaur.
4. We will be going to the races later.

(B) Choose the correct verb for these sentences.
1. Next year he (will grow / grew) about five centimetres.
2. I (hope / hoped) I get a new bike for my birthday.
3. Yesterday I (bought / will buy) a new dress.
4. We (danced / dance) all night at the party.

Adverbs

An adverb describes a verb. Adverbs describe how, when, and where.

Many adverbs, but not all, end in **ly**. Many of these words are adjectives with **ly added.**
Example:
  The choir sang **beautifully.**
  I left **yesterday.**
  They went **outside** to play.

Activity
Underline the adverbs in the following sentences.
1. The man was walking slowly.
2. The batsman was easily confused when the bowlers bowled quickly and then bowled more slowly.
3. The music was playing loudly and had to be turned down.
4. The boy in lane four swam the fastest, while the boy in lane seven was the slowest.

Pronouns

Pronouns are words that we use instead of a noun.
Example:
  I will leave soon.
  They are going to the movies.
  She is studying hard for the exam.

Some pronouns show ownership. These pronouns never have an apostrophe.
Example:
  The dog played with **its** ball.
  Our house is over there.
  That bag is **hers.**

Activity
Underline the pronouns in the following sentences:
1. He is going to do the work straight away.
2. We are all going to the shops so we can buy a present for my sister.
3. Our dog is very sick because they gave her something to eat which she shouldn't have eaten.
4. Their house is next door to yours and I will be moving near you very soon.

Prepositions

Prepositions show a connection between a noun or pronoun and the other words in a sentence. They are usually found in front of the noun or pronoun.

Example:

He is **near** the area now.

The bird flew **over** the house.

Don't go **in** the cave.

Activity

Underline the prepositions in the following sentences:

1. They drove across the bridge .
2. We had to stop the car to see the view of the mountains
3. We went into the house.
4. I gave the book to the teacher.

Articles

There are three words that are articles. They are:
the, a, an.
We use **an** when the next word, normally a noun, starts with a vowel.

Activity
Underline the articles in the following sentences:
1. We went straight to bed when the babysitter told us.
2. The boys gave a wonderful display of skill to the appreciative crowd.
3. The class is going on an excursion to the Jenolan Caves during the second term.
4. A large elephant escaped from the zoo and is walking in a straight line towards the town.

Interjections

Interjections are words that interrupt a conversation and are usually followed by an exclamation mark.

Example:

Oops! I spilled the glass.

The mouse scurried across the floor. **"Eeek!"** screamed the lady.

Activity

Underline the interjections in the following
  sentences:

1. Oh no! cried the coach when the opposition scored their goal.
2. The boy shouted "Hey!" at the two boys trying to break into the shop.
3. Wow! What a great goal.
4. "Hi! Have you been waiting very long for me?" asked John

Punctuation

Punctuation is a collection of symbols that we use in our writing. It is these symbols that make sense of our writing and enable the reader to understand what is written.

Example:

james was in trouble again he was sitting outside the headmasters office come in james said mr jefferies the headmaster what have you done this time i didnt do it said james didnt do what asked the headmaster what ever im here for replied james

This is very difficult to read. However, when it is written with punctuation it becomes much clearer.

James was in trouble again. He was sitting outside the Headmaster's office.
"Come in James," said Mr Jefferies, the Headmaster. "What have you done this time?"
"I didn't do it," said James.
"Didn't do what?" asked the Headmaster.
"What ever I'm here for," replied James.

It is obvious why punctuation is needed. This section will give you a good background in the different types of punctuation and how and when they should be used.

Capital Letters

The first letter of a sentence always starts with a capital letter.

Example:
Are we leaving soon?
The boy went home.
"Hello," welcomed the boy.

Activity (a)
Rewrite these sentences by placing a capital letter at the start of each sentence.

1. a ship crashed into the jagged rocks.

_____

2. don't go near the edge.

_____

3. will you come with me?

_____

4. david won the game easily.

_____

The first letter of a word in quotation marks is also a capital letter. However, if the sentence is broken and has not been completed, then the second part of the sentence does not start with a capital letter.

Example:

"Can you come to the cricket tomorrow?" asked John.

"Don't do that," screamed the instructor, "it's dangerous."

"We went shopping yesterday," explained Helen.

Activity (b)

Punctuate these sentences correctly.

1. "when is it my turn on the computer?" Mary asked.

_____

2. "when you have finished," said Jerry, "come and see me."

_____

3. The police yelled out, "stop that man!"

_____

4. "bill," called his mother, "please clean your room."

_____

The first letter of all proper nouns start with a capital letter.

Example:

James went to **Melbourne** for his holiday.
The play was written by the **Headmaster**.
Katrina played the flute with great passion.

Activity (c)

Rewrite these sentences by giving each proper noun a capital letter.

1. steven dived into the cold water of the atlantic ocean.

_____

2. The coldest months of the year are june, july and august.

_____

3. Did mr smith go with your father to the station?

_____

4. The hume highway is a very dangerous stretch of road.

_____

The main words in the title of a book, film, video, poem, song or play also begin with a capital letter.
Example:
   The story **'Cinderella'** is a fairy tale.
   'The Lion King' is showing at the movies.
   'Advance Australia Fair' is our national song.

The pronoun **I** is always a capital letter.
Example:
   I will be going out later.
   Jason and **I** had a great dinner last night.
   "Can **I** come with you?" asked his little brother.

Activity (d)
Punctuate these sentences.
1. Mary and i went into the shop and bought the latest tracks magazine.
2. Did you see the old James Bond movie, goldfinger on TV last night?
3. i went into the theatre just as the first act of phantom of the opera was starting.
4. i would like a copy of the sydney morning herald, please.

Full stops (.)

A full stop shows the end of a sentence.
Example:
  Here we go again.
  This is my new car.
  The children ran across the street.
A full stop is also used for abbreviations, where the last letter of the abbreviation is different to the last letter of the word.
Example:
  Co. - company
  i.e. - that is
  Rev. - Reverend

A full stop is not used when the last letter of the abbreviation is the same as the last letter of the word.
Example:
  Rd - Road
  Mr - Mister
  Dr - Doctor

A full stop is not used when a number of words has been shortened.
Example:
  USA - United States of America
  ACT - Australian Capital Territory
  QANTAS - Queensland and Northern Territory Air Service

Activity

Place a full stop in the correct place for these sentences. Be careful not to put in full stops when they are not needed, especially in abbreviations.

1. Dr Green was in a very good mood all day yesterday
2. We visited the Mt Piper Power Station during our visit to Hill End
3. Col Davis was in charge of one the AIF battalions during the war
4. Could you please go to the church and ask Rev Stevens if he is going to SA for the meeting

Question Mark (?)

Question marks are placed at the end of the question and are used whenever a question is asked.

Example:

Are you leaving soon?

"Will you have the work finished," asked the teacher, "by the due date?"

How much does a loaf of bread cost?

Activity

Place a question mark at the end of the sentences that are questions.

1. Have you seen my football
2. May I borrow a pencil
3. I saw a mouse over there
4. He asked if he could have some paper

5. Will you come to my place this afternoon
6. James said I could have it
7. When was the last time I went to the cricket
8. Did you leave early from the party

Exclamation Mark (!)

An exclamation mark is used when the writer wants to show a strong feeling. The feeling may be anger, disgust, surprise, excitement, disappointment.
Example:
   "Look out!" screamed the instructor.
   Ouch!
   "Charge!" yelled the Captain.

Activity
Place an exclamation mark at the end of the sentences that are exclamations or after an interjection.
1. I cried, "Look out"
 2. Stop that
3. Will you go away
4. Wow , you've got a great job Michael
5. Oh no, you have broken it
6. Are you leaving
7. We will miss you
8. What a great bike

Commas (,)

Commas are used to show a pause. They are used:
*To separate items in a list.
Example:
   Lisa was given a baby doll, a playdo set, clothes,
   some books and a sun hat for Christmas.
Activity (a)
Place a comma in the correct place to separate these
items.
1. I had to go to the shop and buy bananas apples a
   mango some tomatoes and an apple.
2. I made sure I packed my jumper jeans underwear
   socks shoes and toothbrush.
3. Could you get a newspaper milk bread and eggs
   from the shop.
4. The classroom's projector radio computer were
   taken with some money from the teacher's desk.

* To separate adjectives in a list.
Example:
   The large, long, green table was placed outside.
   The old, worthless book was burned.

Activity (b)
Place a comma in the correct place to separate these
adjectives.
1. The two bright yellow canaries sang very loudly.
2. The small dirty baby appeared to be sleeping.
3. A dusty blue ute pulled into the small township.
4. The new spacious house had a rustic feel to it.

* To separate phrases and clauses in a sentence. Sometimes commas are used to add extra information.

Example:

Our headmaster, Mr Jones, gave a moving speech at the ANZAC Day service.
Andrew, who has just been selected in the state soccer team, is going to give us a demonstration.

The words within the commas give extra information. The sentence would still make sense if they were not included.

Activity (c)

Place a comma in the correct place for these sentences.
1. Mr Jones the music teacher was away today.
2. Our soccer team the Eagles were undefeated this year.
3. The plumber David went under the house.
4. My favourite television show Wide World of Sports is not on TV anymore.

* Before a conjunction.

Example:

We were on our way to the movies, but John decided we should go out for dinner instead.

* After however.

Example:

However, he is going to have to work more consistently.

* In direct speech.

Example:
   "Don't be late," shouted Sally.
   "I won't," called back Michelle, "I'll be there in a minute".

Activity (d)
Place the commas in the correct places for these sentences.
1. Kyle is a large boy but needs to ensure that he doesn't try to use his size for bullying.
2. I enjoyed the show. However I would have liked to get out of the theatre more quickly.
3. "Please don't come any closer" shouted the scared patient.
4. "Hurry" said Tom "or we will be late".

Quotation Marks (" ")

Quotation marks, sometimes called inverted commas, are used to show words spoken. This is often called direct speech. Either double (" ") or single (' ') quotation marks can be used, as long the same type is used throughout the piece of writing.

Example:

"Are you allowed to come out and play?" asked Michael.

"I went shopping, had my hair cut," replied Jenny, "and then went to the beach."

Mum answered, "No, you can't go."

Activity (a)

Place quotation marks in these sentences to show direct speech. You will also need to include commas and full stops, question marks or exclamation marks.

1. Will you be coming soon asked Anne
2. The bags are by the corner replied the teacher
3. What a great place shouted Karen
4. I'll be leaving soon answered the student

Quotation marks are not used in indirect speech.

Example:

Matthew said he wanted to come.

Quotation marks are also used for titles of books, television programmes, videos, songs, plays and poems. If the title appears within direct speech then different quotation marks are used to the ones showing direct speech.

Example:
I was given the new book, 'The Shane Warne
Factor', for Christmas.
"Would you like to come to the movies and see
'The Lion King'?" asked Robert.
We had to study 'Macbeth' for our HSC.

Activity (b)
Place quotation marks, and any other punctuation
missing, in the correct places in these sentences
1. Can we get the video Surfing Australia for our
   birthdays asked the boys
2. I use the Macquarie Dictionary all the time
3. Have you seen A Current Affair tonight
4. Can I have your copy of The Merchant of Venice

* The final use of quotation marks is to indicate
  direct quotations.If the quote appears within direct
  speech then different quotation marks are used to
  the ones showing direct speech.

Example:
"Then this loud voice spoke, 'Leave now!', so we
left immediately," reported Sandra.
"I heard them ask, 'Is that the one?'," said Allison.
"Let sleeping dogs lie" is a well known proverb.

Activity (c)
Place quotation marks and any other punctuation in
the correct places for the following sentences.
1. The proverb too many cooks spoil the broth is
   often correct
2.Garry reported to New Idea that the Queen Mother

sleeps with her dogs

3. John asked have you seen my Yellow Submarine single around

4. One great quote from the war was I will be back by General MacArthur

Apostrophes (')

Apostrophes have three uses. The first is to show that one or more letters have been left out of a word. This is called a contraction.

Example:

They're going to the beach with Michelle and her mum. (they are)

I felt really sorry for Rhonda because she **couldn't** come to the party. (could not)

I've had enough. (I have)

Activity

(a) Write the contractions for these words. Remember to put the apostrophe where the missing letters are.

1. it is _____   2. did not _____

3. will not _____   4. can not _____

(b) Write the words these contractions stand for:

1. shan't _____   2. he'll _____

3. we've _____   4. you're _____

The second use of apostrophes is to show ownership or possession. We do this by placing an apostrophe and an **s** after the owner. It can be confusing sometimes to decide where to place the apostrophe, especially if the last letter of the owner is an **s.** If you follow this rule you will not make mistakes. Ask yourself who is the owner and then place the apostrophe after the last letter of the owner.

Example:
Is this Kylie's hat?
That red and white bag is Megan's.
The children's clothes all need cleaning.
The swimmers' bus is running very late.
Mr Thompson's computer was stolen last night.

Activity (c)
Place an apostrophe in the correct place to show ownership.
1. Davids house is over there.
2. Where are the class' clothes?
3. Have you seen Mr Millers shoes?
4. This is Janes book, where is Kylies?

The last use of apostrophes is for writing plurals of numbers or letters.

Example:
  The batsman scored eight 4's and two 6's in his innings.
  Is this 10 B's netball team?
  How many 6's in 42?
  Mind your p's and q's.
  He was a great hockey player in the 1980's.

Activity (d)
Place an apostrophe in the correct place for these sentences.
1. I made the 11Cs this year.
2. How many As did you get on your report card?
3. Did you know that there are twelve 12s in one hundred and forty-four.
4. Make sure all the Under 14s get their trophies.

Apostrophe Revision

Activity
Place an apostrophe in the correct place for these sentences.
1. Did you hear that Jennys report card had two Cs?
2. Wont you come and play with the Year 6s?

Sentence Structure

It is important to understand how sentences are formed correctly. This knowledge will help ensure that your writing is grammatically correct.

Sentences

A sentence is a group of words that make sense and contains a finite verb. All sentences begin with a capital letter and end with a full stop, question mark or exclamation mark.

There are four different types of sentences, statement, question, command and explanation.

Example:
  I enjoy riding my bike. (Statement)
  Is that your book? (Question)
  Come here now. (Command)
  Look out! (Exclamation)

Activity
Decide if these sentences are statements, questions, commands or exclamations by placing a **s, q, c** or **e** after the sentence.
1. Did you come last night?
2. I went to the beach yesterday.
3. Go to the office.
4. I don't want to go!

Phrases

A phrase is a group of words that does not have a finite verb and does not make sense by itself. A phrase must start with a preposition and adds meaning or description to the sentence.

Example
  in the red car
  in the sea
  at the beach
  by midnight

Activity
Underline the phrases in these sentences.
1. We went to the oval.
2. I went for a ride.
3. We should have gone by bus.
4. Jane sat under a tree.

Clauses

A clause is a group of words that has a finite verb and its subject.

Example
The boys are swimming.
You can't go!
The bus is late.
Can we come?

Activity
Underline the clause by finding the finite verb and its subject in these sentences.
1. The mouse chased the cat.
2. We all went running.
3. The book was damaged.
4. I left school yesterday.

Answers

Parts of Speech

Common nouns

1. We went to the <u>beach</u> and played with the <u>ball</u>.
2. The <u>boy</u> climbed over the <u>gate</u> and was chased by a <u>bull</u>.
3. The <u>girls</u> had a <u>party</u> to celebrate leaving <u>school</u>.
4. Each <u>chair</u> had to have a matching <u>cushion</u>.

Proper nouns

1. <u>Jenny</u> and <u>David</u> took their younger brother to <u>Taronga Zoo</u>.
2. <u>Captain Cook</u> explored much of the <u>South Pacific Ocean</u> and discovered the east coast of <u>Australia</u>.
3. The fire surrounded the tiny township of <u>Louth</u>.
4. <u>Elton John</u> will be performing at the <u>Sydney Entertainment Centre</u> tonight.

Collective nouns

1. The <u>swarm</u> of bees buzzed around my head.
2. The <u>school</u> of fish were all caught in the net.
3. The <u>battalion</u> charged the enemy and suffered many casualties.
4. The <u>pride</u> of lions looked harmless but the <u>crowd</u> knew they would attack if they disturbed them.

Abstract nouns

1. The boys had a lot of <u>fun</u> at Luna Park on Saturday.
2. We had no <u>idea</u> who committed the murder in the video until right at the end.
3. It is a <u>pity</u> we had to leave early.
4. The <u>exhilaration</u> we felt as we plummeted down the roller coaster was indescribable.

Noun Revision

            C   C   C

a) 1. The young <u>boy</u> sent his <u>friend</u> a new <u>comic</u> for

      C

his <u>birthday</u>.

            P   C   Col

2. The <u>Headmaster</u> gave a <u>talk</u> to the <u>class</u> about

     A

<u>honesty</u>.

      P   C   Col

3. <u>Mr Jones</u> was a <u>butcher</u> and bought a <u>chain</u> of

  C   P

<u>stores</u> called <u>Pete's Meat</u>.

b) Soldiers fight to ensure we have **freedom**.
A neighbour of Australia is **Indonesia**.
We camp in a **tent**.
A **squadron** of aeroplanes.

Adjectives

1. The <u>seven</u> girls went out for dinner and came home very late.
2. The <u>shiny</u> <u>red</u> convertible sped along the <u>new</u> highway.
3. The <u>third</u> boy was totally exhausted, but he ignored the <u>extreme</u> pain and finished the race.
4. The <u>young</u> boy wanted a <u>new</u> <u>mountain</u> bike for his tenth birthday.

Simple and Compound Verbs

1. The train <u>chugged</u>[S] along the tracks as the thieves <u>rode</u>[S] their horses alongside.

2. He <u>will be allowed</u>[C] to go <u>out</u>[C] tonight.

3. Dad <u>has made</u>[C] me a new cubby house.

4. Both our school teams <u>were beaten</u>[C] in the first round.

Finite Verb

1. The boy <u>rode</u> his bike down the hill. *(S above rode)*

2. The boat <u>sank</u> very quickly. *(S above sank)*

3. Katherine <u>came</u> to the library with me. *(S above came)*

4. We <u>smashed</u> through the barrier. *(S above smashed)*

Tense

i) 1. The boy <u>sang</u> beautifully. (**past**)
2. The girls <u>are playing</u> water polo. (**present**)
3. The excavators <u>discovered</u> a fossil of a dinosaur. (**past**)
4. We <u>will be going</u> to the races later. (**future**)

ii) 1. Next year he (**will grow** / ~~grew~~) about five centimetres.
2. I (**hope** / ~~hoped~~) I get a new bike for my birthday.
3. Yesterday I (**bought** / ~~will buy~~) a new dress.
4. We (**danced** / ~~dance~~) all night at the party.

Adverbs

1. The man was walking <u>slowly</u>.
2. The batsman was <u>easily</u> confused when the bowlers bowled <u>quickly</u> and then bowled <u>more slowly</u>.
3. The music was playing <u>loudly</u> and had to be turned <u>down</u>.
4. The boy in lane four swam the <u>fastest</u>, while the boy in lane seven was the <u>slowest</u>.

Pronouns

1. <u>He</u> is going to do the work straight away.
2. <u>We</u> are all going to the shops so <u>we</u> can buy a present for <u>my</u> sister.
3. <u>Our</u> dog is very sick because <u>they</u> gave <u>her</u> something to eat which <u>she</u> shouldn't have eaten.
4. <u>Their</u> house is next door to <u>yours</u> and <u>I</u> will be moving near <u>you</u> very soon.

Prepositions

1. They drove <u>across</u> the bridge.
2. We had to stop the car to see the view <u>of</u> the mountains.
3. We went <u>into</u> the house.
4. I gave the book <u>to</u> the teacher.

Articles

1. We went straight to bed when <u>the</u> babysitter told us.
2. <u>The</u> boys gave <u>a</u> wonderful display of skill to <u>the</u> appreciative crowd.
3. <u>The</u> class is going on <u>an</u> excursion to <u>the</u> Jenolan Caves during <u>the</u> second term.
4. <u>A</u> large elephant escaped from <u>the</u> zoo and is walking in <u>a</u> straight line towards <u>the</u> town.

Interjections

1. <u>Oh no</u>! cried the coach when the opposition scored their goal.
2. The boy shouted "<u>Hey</u>!" at the two boys trying to

break into the shop.

3. <u>Wow</u>! What a great goal.

4. "<u>Hi</u>! Have you been waiting very long for me?" asked John.

Punctuation

Capital Letters

(a) 1. **A** ship crashed into the jagged rocks.

2. **Don't** go near the edge.

3. **Will** you come with me?

4. **David** won the game easily.

(b) 1. "**When** is it my turn on the computer?" Mary asked.

2. "**When** you have finished," said Jerry, "come and see me."

3. The police yelled out, "**Stop** that man!"

4. "**Bill**," called his mother, "please clean your room."

(c) 1. **Steven** dived into the cold water of the **A**tlantic **O**cean.

2. The coldest months of the year are **June, July** and **August**.

3. Did **Mr Smith** go with your father to the station?

4. The **Hume Highway** is a very dangerous stretch of road.

(d) 1. Mary and **I** went into the shop and bought the latest 'Tracks' magazine.

2. Did you see the old James Bond movie, "Goldfinger" on TV last night?

3. I went into the theatre just as the first act of "Phantom of the Opera" was starting.
4. I would like a copy of "The Sydney Morning Herald," please.

Full Stops

1. Dr Green was in a very good mood all day yesterday.
2. We visited the Mt. Piper Power Station during our visit to Hill End.
3. Col Davis was in charge of one the AIF battalions during the war.
4. Could you please go to the church and ask Rev. Stevens if he is going to SA for the meeting.

Question Marks

1. Have you seen my football?
2. May I borrow a pencil?
3. I saw a mouse over there.
4. He asked if he could have some paper.
5. Will you come to my place this afternoon?
6. James said I could have it.
7. When was the last time I went to the cricket?
8. Did you leave early from the party?

Exclamation Marks

1. I cried, "Look out!"
2. Stop that !
3. Will you go away!
4. Wow!, you've got a great job Michael.
5. Oh no!, you have broken it .

6. Are you leaving?

7. We will miss you! or .**(The answer will depend on the emphasis the reader gives)**

8. What a great bike! or .**(The answer will depend on the emphasis the reader gives)**

Commas

(a) 1. I had to go to the shop and buy bananas, apples, a mango, some tomatoes and an apple.

2. I made sure I packed my jumper, jeans, underwear, socks, shoes and toothbrush.

3. Could you get a newspaper, milk, bread and eggs from the shop.

4. The classroom's projector, radio and computer were taken with some money from the teacher's desk.

(b) 1. The two, bright, yellow canaries sang very loudly.

2. The small, dirty baby appeared to be sleeping.

3. A dusty, blue ute pulled into the small township.

4. The new, spacious house had a rustic feel to it.

(c) 1. Mr Jones, the music teacher, was away today.

2. Our soccer team, the Eagles, were undefeated this year.

3. The plumber, David, went under the house.

4. My favourite television show, "Wide World of Sports", is not on TV anymore.

(d) 1. Kyle is a large boy, but needs to ensure that he doesn't try to use his size for bullying.

2. I enjoyed the show. However, I would have liked to get out of the theatre more quickly.

3. "Please don't come any closer," shouted the scared patient.

4. "Hurry," said Tom, "or we will be late".

Quotation Marks

(a) 1. "Will you be coming soon?" asked Anne.
    2. "The bags are by the corner," replied the teacher.
    3. "What a great place!" shouted Karen.
    4. "I'll be leaving soon," answered the student.
(b) 1. "Can we get the video 'Surfing Australia' for our birthdays," asked the boys.
    2. I use the 'Macquarie Dictionary' all the time.
    3. Have you seen 'A Current Affair' tonight?
    4. "Can I have your copy of 'The Merchant of Venice'."
(c) 1. The proverb, 'Too many cooks spoil the broth', is often correct.
    2. Garry reported to 'New Idea' that the Queen Mother sleeps with her dogs.
    3. John asked, "Have you seen my 'Yellow Submarine' single around? "
    4. One great quote from the war was, "I will be back" by General MacArthur.

Apostrophes

(a)   1. it 's   2. didn't   3. won't   4. can't
(b)   1. shall not 2. he will   3. we have 4. you are
(c)   1. David's house is over there.
    2. Where are the class' clothes?
    3. Have you seen Mr Miller's shoes?
    4. This is Jane's book, where is Kylie's?
(d)   1. I made the 11C's this year.
    2. How many A's did you get on your report card?

3. Did you know that there are twelve 12's in one hundred and forty-four.
4. Make sure all the Under 14's get their trophies.

Apostrophe Revision

1. Did you hear that Jenny's report card had two C's?
2. Won't you come and play with the Year 6's?

Sentences

1. Did you come last night? **Question**
2. I went to the beach yesterday. **Statement**
3. Go to the office. **Command**
4. I don't want to go! **Exclamation**

Phrases

1. We went <u>to the oval</u>.
2. I went <u>for a ride</u>.
3. We should have gone <u>by bus</u>.
4. Jane sat <u>under a tree</u>.

Clauses

1. <u>The mouse chased the cat</u>.
2. <u>We all went running</u>.
3. <u>The book was damaged</u>.
4. <u>I left school</u> yesterday.